Millie Sue and Her Friends

(who all want to be big right away)

Written and Illustrated by

Carleen Schomberg

For my Grandchildren

Millie Sue was a wee tadpole
and she was feeling blue.
She said, "Mom, you are so pretty,
but I don't look like you."

Mom said, "Don't worry, Millie.
Your tail will disappear.
You'll be a gorgeous frog one day.
Now don't you fret, my dear."

"You're going to grow some fine, strong legs
and they'll be great for hoppin'.
We'll get ourselves all prettied-up
and take ourselves fly shoppin'.

We'll hop about on lily pads
and croak beneath the moon.
But, for now, enjoy your tadpole time.
You'll grow up all too soon."

Little Freddie-Small-Fry
    was swimming in a pool
        with all the other little fish
            who go to Freddie's school.

    But Freddie was impatient
        to swim out on his own.
            He didn't want to wait around
                until he was full grown.

"Hold on there, Son", advised his dad.
It's not your time to go
into the open ocean
with creatures you don't know.

Out in the deeper water,
some dine on little fish.
And you're so small and tender,
You'd make a tasty dish."

"But you'll be big enough real soon
to swim from sea to sea.
For now, though, I'm so happy
you're here to play with me!"

Tommy Tortoise dragged his feet
  and plodded through the sand.
    "Mom, I must go fast," he said.
      "Could you lend me a hand?

I want to gather up some speed
  and join the lizard's race.
    But, even when I try real hard,
      I can't pick up the pace."

"Don't be sad, my little buddy.
        You are perfect as you are."
            Said his mother, smiling proudly,
                "You were built to travel far.

With your house upon your back,
        you can wander far and wide.
            And if ever there is danger,
                you can tuck yourself inside."

Sarah Sparrow, upon a branch,
     looked down and spied a cat.
          "If I was a mighty eagle," she peeped,
               "I would not put up with that!

I'd swoop down and teach that kitty
     not to chase and swat at me.
          Oh, I wish I were an eagle,
               not a sparrow in a tree."

"Don't be silly," said her sister.
    We can flit from yard to yard.
        For an eagle, who can't do that,
            finding food is very hard.

We are brave, and cute, and tiny
    and we don't have many needs.
        And some kind, good-hearted people
            hang up feeders filled with seeds.

Of all the animals on earth,
    I think we are the best.
        We can fly, and glide, and sing, and hop,
            then come home to our nest."

Faye the Fawn was nibbling grass
    in a meadow, near the shade.
        She was wishing she were bigger
            so she wouldn't be afraid.

She said, "Dad, I worry so
    about big cats and men who hunt.
        I wish I wasn't such a timid,
            trembling little runt."

Father said, "Come here, My Precious,
    for I have a tale to tell.
        Your mom and I will keep you close
           and warm and safe and well.

As you grow, you'll feel much braver,
    and you'll come to understand –
        you are the deer – most graceful one
           to ever roam the land."

"Each creature has a special part
    to play upon the earth,
        and each receives a special gift
           the moment of his birth.

Some have speed, or strength, or heart.
    Some courage, love or grace.
        When all of us have room to grow,
           the earth's a better place."

Trafford rev. 12/23/2019

 www.trafford.com
North America & international
toll-free: 1 888 232 4444 (USA & Canada)
fax: 812 355 4082

Printed in the United States
By Bookmasters